AF481417

Hex codes, or hexadecimal codes, are a way to represent colors in digital devices and web design. Each hex code refers to a very specific color. A hex color is expressed as a six-digit combination of numbers and letters, preceded by a pound sign or hashtag, defined by its mix of red, green, and blue (RGB). The first two letters or numbers refer to red, the next two refer to green, and the last two refer to blue.

The color values are defined as values between 00 and FF. Hex codes are a universal way to describe colors. This book is specifically about shades of red.

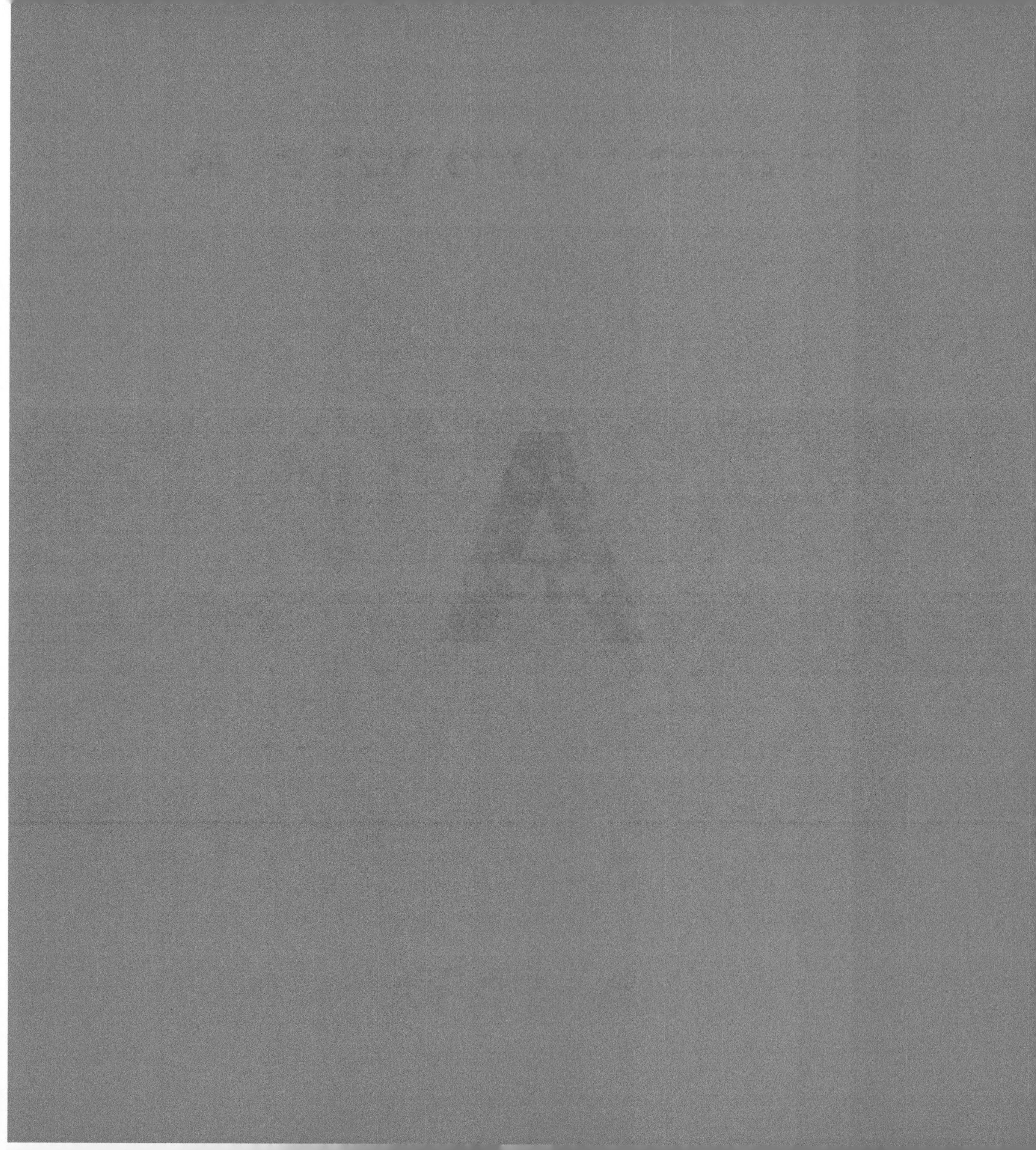

B is for barn red

B

#7C0A02

C is for candy apple

#FF0800

c is for crimson

C

#B80F0A

D is for dark red

D

#8B000

d is for desire

d

#EA3C53

E is for electric crimson

E

#FF003F

e is for english red

e

#AB4B52

G is for geranium red

G

#F04B51

g is for glitterbug

g

#A93A37

H is for hawthorn

#F7060D

h is for holly berry

h

#C00000

I is for ink red

I

#550000

i is for iron oxide

#B63730

J is for jasper red

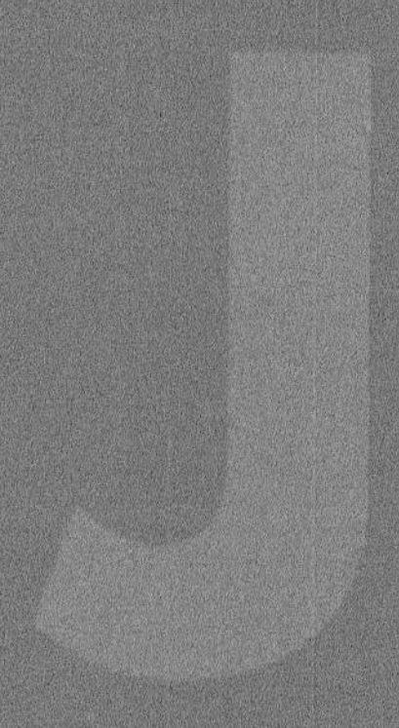

#D73B3E

j is for jelly bean red

#DA614E

K is for kermes

#DC143C

k is for ketchup

#B50000

L is for laser red

#E2221D

l is for lava

#CF1020

M is for madder red

M

#A50021

m is for munsell red

m

#F2003C

N is for naphthol red
N
#BE2D39

n is for nebula 2
#C92442

O is for old brick

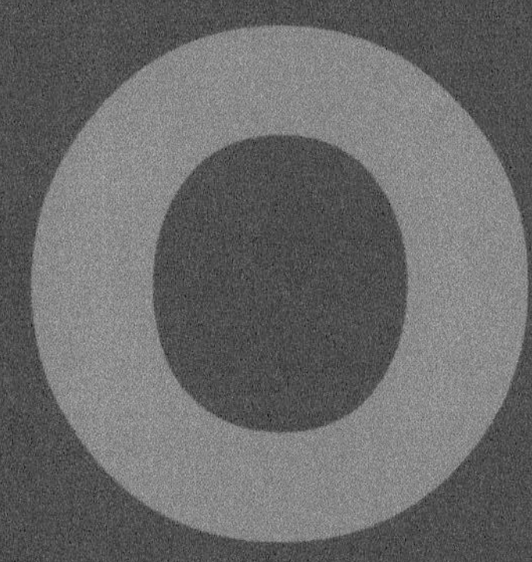

#901E1E

o is for opium red

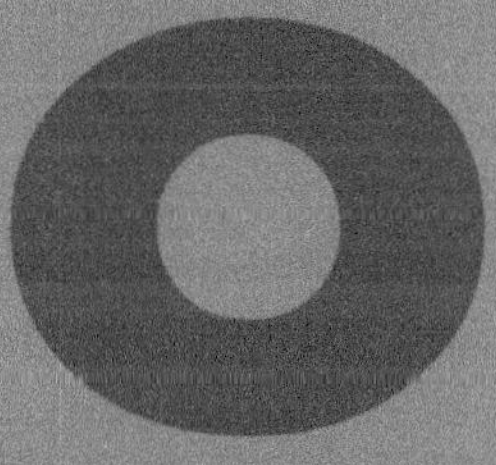

#F04F57

P is for pastel red

P

#FF6961

p is for pigment red

p

#B40E26

R is for radical red

R

#FF355E

r is for rusty red

#DA2C43

S is for sangria

S

#92000A

s is for sanguine red

s

#BC3F4A

T is for tall poppy

#B32D29

t is for tamarillo

#991613

U is for up maroon

U

#7B1113

u is for upsdell red

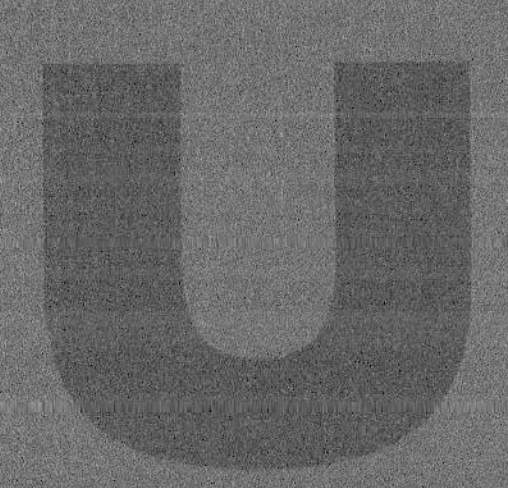

#AE2029

V is for venetian red

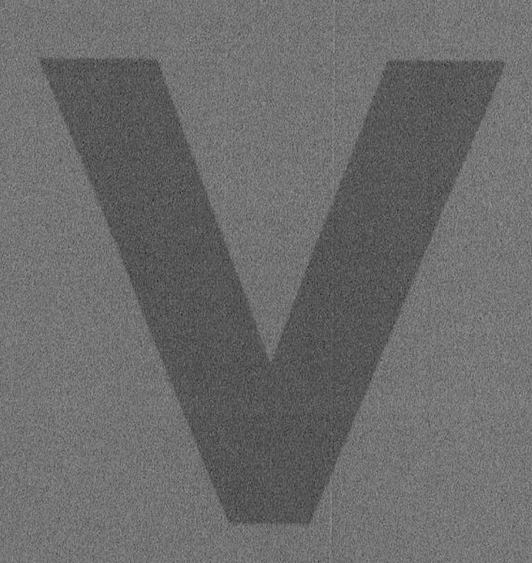

#C80815

v is for vibe

V

#AC3142

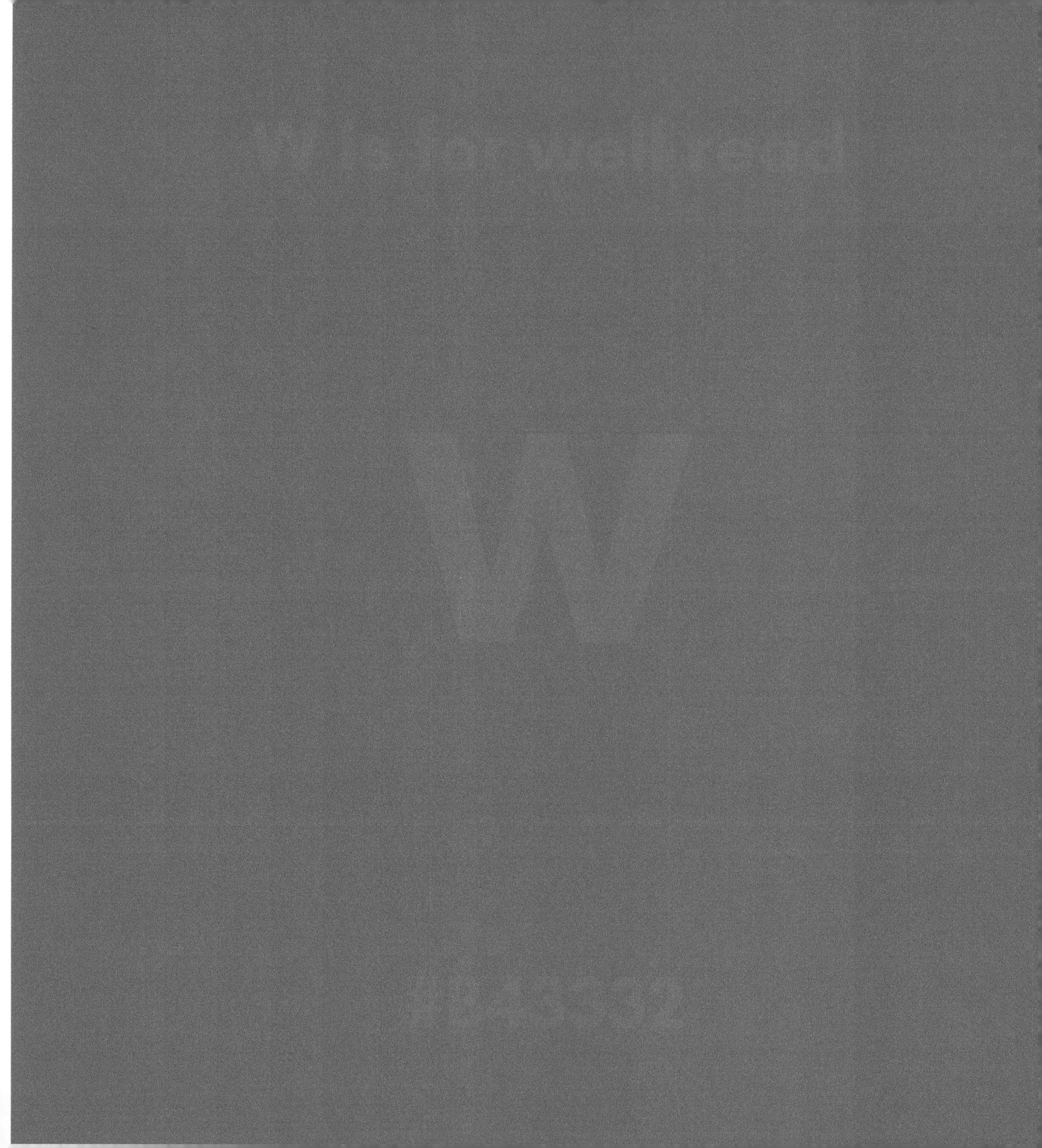

w is for well sausage

W

#BB3A24

X is for x factor

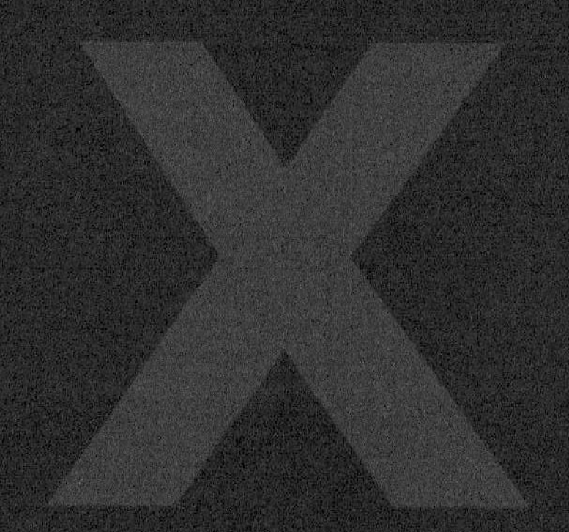

#681B2B

x is for xl roasted red pepper

#87393B

Y is for yaquil trail

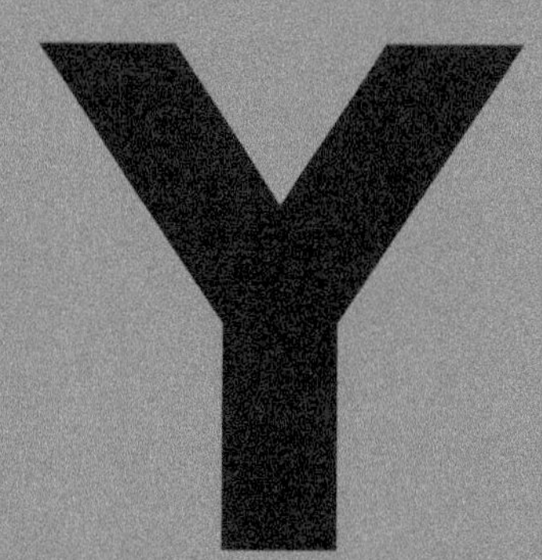

#C48178

y is for yen red

y

#330000

Z is for zesty

Z

#BA4D3C

z is for zinger

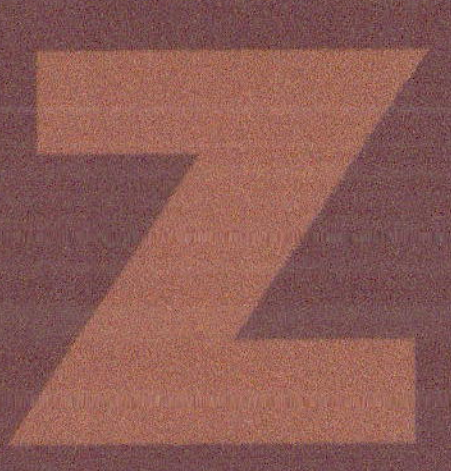

#873D42